POCKET GUIDE TO

WHALES, DOLPHINS
AND. OTHER
MARINE MAMMALS

Lincoln
Children's Books

WELCOME TO THIS BOOK!

In this book, you will learn all about the wonderful world of marine mammals. Here's how to navigate the pages.

Six chapter headers introduce you to the main marine mammal groups.

SEALS & WALRUS

Seals and sea lions are sleek and streamlined underwater swimmers that can perform underwater acrobatics. They have two pairs of large flippers used for swimming and are clumsy walkers on land. They have a small, inconspicuous tail, are covered in thick fur, and have long whiskers on their snout.

Here are the seals!

Family and species spreads let you go into more depth. Not every species or family is listed in this book, as there are too many to fit. This selection should give you an idea of the wide variety of marine life on Earth.

Group name

Family name

Number of species in that group

Example species

Learn more about this species in "A Closer Look"

"Did You Know?" boxes give more information on the species and the group

TRUE SEALS

family name
Phocidae

number of species
18

While they are expert swimmers, true seals are very ungainly on land. In the water, they sweep their powerful hind flippers from side to side just as a fish does with its tail. On land these flippers trail behind them and they drag themselves forward using their front flippers. True seals have excellent hearing even though they are sometimes called earless seals. Their ears are almost invisible with just a tiny entrance hole behind each eye.

Harbor seal

▶▶▶ EXAMPLE: HARBOR SEAL (Phoca vitulina) ◀◀◀

SWIMMING
Baby harbor seals can swim almost right away after they are born. They shed their white baby fur while they are inside their mother, and their ...w fur is pale gray and waterproof. They need to swim quickly because they are often born on sand ...nks where the tide comes back in soon after they are born.

A CLOSER LOOK

» **LIFESPAN**
25 years (males)
35 years (females)

» **SIZE**
Up to ... ft

» **WEIGHT**
...to 330 lb

» **DIET**
Fish, squid, octopus, crabs, and other crustaceans

» **CONSERVATION STATUS**
Least Concern. About 500,000 worldwide.

» **LOCATION**
Near coasts in N. Atlantic, North Pacific, and Arctic

DID YOU KNOW?
• Some harbor seals in San Francisco Bay have red fur. Iron stirred up from the seabed colors their fur so they look rusty.

• Harbor seals often swim up rivers.

• Harbor seals can stay underwater for up to 30 minutes, but an average dive is around three minutes.

• True seals produce milk that is 40–60% fat so the young grow very quickly. harbor seal milk is about 50% fat.

This side of the page tells you about an animal family in this group. Here is the true seal family.

This side of the page shows you one amazing creature from this family: the harbor seal!

LIFE ON EARTH

No one knows how many different kinds of living things there are on Earth. So far, nearly two million have been named—and we call each of these a "species." A species is a group of plants, animals, fungi, or microorganisms that look similar and are able to breed with each other.

New species are being discovered all the time. There

are estimated to be at least six and a half million still waiting to be found (not even counting bacteria and other microbes). Most of these will be tiny, but in 2002 a new species of whale more than 10 feet long, called Perrin's beaked whale, was found in California!

All living species, from tir bacteria to huge whales a made up of microscopic "building blocks" called cells. Some have only one while others have billions. All life-forms share a nee for energy stored in food so that they can live, grov and reproduce.

CLASSIFICATION

When scientists describe a new species they give it a unique scientific name. This has two parts, the genus name and the species name. For example, the North Atlantic right whale is called *Eubalaena glacialis*, and no other living thing on Earth has this name. The southern right whale (*Eubalaena australis*) is closely related and so is grouped in the same genus: *Eubalaena*. Scientific names are useful because they are the same in whatever language you speak.

All known living things are arranged into groups. First, they are put into really huge groups called kingdoms and then into smaller and smaller groups until the smallest division, which is the individual species. The chart on the right shows you how to classify a West Indian manatee.

KINGDOM: ANIMALIA
This kingdom includes all animals.

PHYLUM: CHORDATA
This includes all animals that have a backbone.

CLASS: MAMMALIA
A class is a group of orders that share similar characteristics.

ORDER: Sirenia
An order contains closely related animal families.

FAMILY: Trichechidae
A family includes closely related genera (plural of genus).

GENUS: *Trichechus*
A genus contains closely related species.

SPECIES: *Trichechus manatus*
The basic unit whose members can breed with each other.

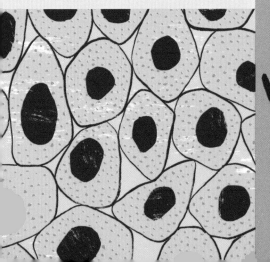

West Indian manatee!

WHAT IS A MAMMAL?

Mammals are a large group of vertebrates (animals with backbones), most of which live on land. Lions, bears, rats, monkeys, whales, seals, and humans are all mammals. There are about 5,500 different mammal species living today, and only about 130 of these live in the ocean. Mammals can be large or small, prickly or soft, brightly colored or drab. The largest land species is the African elephant, but the largest species of all is the blue whale (see pp. 16-17). The smallest is the bumblebee bat. It only weighs 2 grams, which is about half the weight of a sugar lump.

Even though they may look very different from one another, all mammals share two features-they all have hair and they all feed their babies milk. Even dolphins and whales have hair, though only a very few and sometimes only when they are babies.

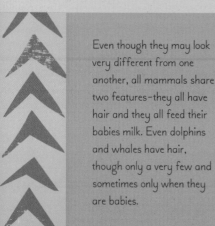

All mammals give bir
live young-except ech
and platypus, which
eggs.

WHAT IS A MARINE MAMMAL?

There are five main groups of marine mammals:
cetaceans (whales, dolphins, and porpoises), otters (sea and marine), sirenians (dugongs and manatees), polar bears, and pinnipeds (sea lions, seals, and walrus).

Cetaceans

Otters

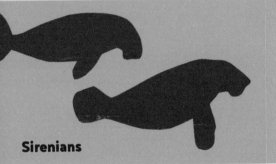

Sirenians

Polar bears

Pinnipeds

True marine mammals get all or at least most of their food from the sea. Cetaceans and sirenians spend their whole lives in water, while pinnipeds, otters, and polar bears come out onto land to have their babies. Some also come ashore to rest or to shed their old hair and grow a new fur coat.

LIFE IN WATER

The ancestors of marine mammals used to live on lan
Slowly, some of these took to living in the ocean. Here, they found new food sources and could escape predators. The five groups of marine mammals evolved separately and at different times. Living in water is very different from living on land, so marine mammals developed specia adaptations to help them swim efficiently, keep warm, and find and eat their food.

Marine mammals do not all share the same ancestors and evolved from different groups of land mammals.

New evidence suggests that cetaceans (whales and dolphins) evolved from a group that today contains hippos and cattle. Sirenians (sea cows) share a common ancestor with elephants and pinnipeds (seals and sea lions) probably had a bear-like ancestor.

ADAPTIONS

Marine mammals breathe air just like other mammals.

To make this easier, cetaceans and sirenians have nostrils on top of their head. They can surface and take a breath without even lifting their head out of the water. Many land mammals can swim, but most marine mammals are also expert deep divers. Some can hold their breath for more than an hour. They do this by storing oxygen in their muscles, as well as in their blood and lungs.

Most marine mammals have lost their hind limbs, the fore limbs have become flippers, and they have large tails. Seals and sea lions have kept their hind limbs as large flippers, while otters and polar bears still have four legs.

Most marine mammals have an insulating layer of blubber beneath the skin, while others have thick, waterproof fur.

Streamlined bodies allow whales, dolphins, and seals to swim fast and easily.

SPOTTING GUIDE

You can find marine mammals living in all the oceans of the world. Some prefer warm water such as the Indian Ocean, while other species are at home in the freezing waters of the Arctic and Southern Oceans. Some species such as orcas (killer whales) are cosmopolitan, which means they are found throughout the world in all oceans. Look at the map below to see where the oceans of the world are.

Arctic Ocean

Atlantic Ocean

Indian Ocean

Pacific Ocean

Southern Ocean

WHICH WATERS?

Most marine mammals live near the coast in fairly shallow water, but cetaceans (whales and dolphins) are found far out to sea as well. Cetaceans will sometimes swim into river estuaries but just three species live their whole lives in freshwater rivers.

With their warm fur coats, pinnipeds (seals and sea lions) live mainly in temperate (cool) parts of the ocean and in icy-cold Arctic and Antarctic waters. Only two species of seals live in fresh water (see p. 51). Pinnipeds live near land so that they can rest on safe beaches called haul-outs. Beaches where they have their babies are called rookeries.

Sirenians (manatees and dugongs) live in tropical waters along coastlines. The dugong is found in the Indian and Western Pacific Oceans and manatees in the Atlantic Ocean. Manatees also live in river systems that empty into the Atlantic, such as the Amazon.

Otters and bears live mainly in fresh water and on land and only sea otters and polar bears rely entirely on the ocean for their food.

BALEEN WHALES

There are 14 species of baleen whale and all of them are huge. Instead of teeth, they have a mouthful of baleen plates, like brushes with long, stiff bristles. These hang down from the upper jaw and trap floating animals such as plankton. All baleen whales have two blowholes on the top of their head.

RIGHT WHALES

family name	number of species
Balaenidae	**3**

Right whales are enormous, fat whales with huge heads and smooth, wide backs. They have a strange mouth shaped like an arch, which is filled with dangling baleen plates. They can be spotted swimming slowly along at the surface with their mouth wide open. Water streams through their fine baleen and tiny crustaceans get trapped. They have lumpy white patches of skin on their head called callosites.

North Atlantic right whale

EXAMPLE: NORTH ATLANTIC RIGHT WHALE *(Eubalaena glacialis)*

ROAD TO RECOVERY

North Atlantic right whales are the rarest of all baleen whales. They were the first whales to be hunted and sold for money. They were chosen as the "right" whale to hunt because they swam slowly near the surface and were easy to catch. There were once only a few hundred of these whales left. But now hunting these creatures is banned, and numbers of North Atlantic right whales are slowly starting to recover.

Callosites

DID YOU KNOW?

* Right whales can dive 600 feet deep and touch the sea floor with their calloused heads.

* When they are at the surface, southern right whales sometimes stick their huge tails in the air and hang upside down for a long time. No one really knows why.

* Scientists can recognize individual right whales from the pattern of their lumpy skin callosities.

* When they feed at the surface, waves knock their baleen plates together, which makes a clicking noise called a "baleen rattle."

A CLOSER LOOK

» LIFESPAN
Up to 70 years old

» SIZE
Up to 60 ft long

» WEIGHT
Up to 90 tons: females are larger than males

» DIET
Zooplankton and krill

» CONSERVATION STATUS
Endangered: there are fewer than 500 left in the world.

» LOCATION
Atlantic waters, often near the coast

RORQUALS

family name	number of species
Balaenopteridae	**8**

Rorquals are shaped like a long torpedo, with a pointed he
and a small fin on the back near their tail. When rorquals fe
they open their mouth, lunge upward, and take a huge gul
of water and krill. They have long pleats in their throat, whi
stretch out and make a bag to hold the water, which they
force through their baleen plates. Then they can swallow th
trapped food. Let's look at two examples of famous rorqua

OCEAN GIANTS

The blue whale is the largest of all whales. It is the longest animal that has ever lived on Earth—even longer than the largest dinosaur. They give birth to live babies, which are 23 to 26 feet long when they are born. The mother feeds them her milk, and it is so rich that they can gain up to 200 pounds in weight a day.

Blow

A CLOSER LOOK

» LIFESPAN
80-90 years

» SIZE
Up to 100 ft

» WEIGHT
Up to 200 tons

» DIET
Small shrimp
called krill

» CONSERVATION STATUS
Endangered; about 10,000-25,000 in the world.

» LOCATION
Worldwide: some make long journeys to feed in cold waters during the summer and breed in tropical waters in the winter

DID YOU KNOW?

★ Blue whales are the only rorquals that are blue-gray. The rest are dark gray or black with some white.

★ Like other rorquals they have a ridge along the head that forms a "splash guard" around the blowholes. The blow can reach 30-40 feet high.

★ Blue whales communicate with hums and moans and have one of the loudest sounds of any animal.

★ Blue whales in the Indian Ocean are shorter—but can be just as heavy. They are called pygmy blue whales.

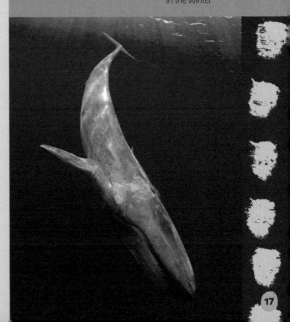

EXAMPLE 2: HUMPBACK WHALE *(Megaptera novaeangliae)*

The humpback is an exceptional rorqual whale. You can tell it is a rorqual because it has throat pleats, but it is much sturdier than the blue whale and has long flippers. These flippers are edged with hard knobs called tubercles, and sharp barnacles often grow on them. Males sometimes use their flippers to hit other males and keep them away from their mate. The flippers show up well underwater because the underside is a bright white.

Humpback whale

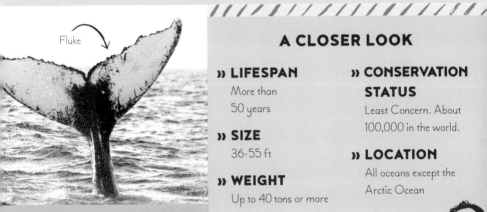

BUBBLE NETS

Rorqual whales usually feed alone on patches of krill, but humpback whales will also eat shoals of small fish. Unlike other rorquals, they often work together and will surround a fish shoal with their hungry mouths. Some humpback groups dive down below a fish shoal and blow bubbles all around it. The fish press close together inside the bubble ring, and the whales take great mouthfuls as they lunge up through them.

Fluke

A CLOSER LOOK

» LIFESPAN
More than 50 years

» SIZE
36-55 ft

» WEIGHT
Up to 40 tons or more

» DIET
Small shrimp called krill and small fish

» CONSERVATION STATUS
Least Concern. About 100,000 in the world.

» LOCATION
All oceans except the Arctic Ocean

DID YOU KNOW?

★ These whales are called humpbacks because there is a hump underneath the fin on their back.

★ Humpbacks are the most acrobatic of all the large whales. They jump right up out of the water and splash back down. They also slap the water with their tails and flippers.

★ Every humpback has a different black-and-white pattern on the underside of its tail.

★ Humpbacks make some of the longest journeys of all whales. They can swim as far as 5,000 miles to find warm tropical waters for the winter. Then they journey back in spring to cold water, where there is more food.

GRAY WHALES

family name	number of species
Eschrichtiidae	**1**

Gray whales are one of the easiest large whales to spot because the
live near the coast and swim quite slowly. Some mother gray whales e
allow their babies to swim right up to small boats. The adults are cove
in pale blotches–especially on their heads. These white blotches ar
actually barnacles and lice that live stuck to the whales' skin.

Gray whale

GREAT MIGRATION

Gray whales live in the North Pacific Ocean. In the summer, they feed around Alaska, where there is plenty of food. As winter approaches, they swim south to the warm waters of Baja California in Mexico. Their babies (calves) are born here. When they are only a few weeks old, the calves must swim back with their mothers, on an incredible journey of more than 6,000 miles.

A CLOSER LOOK

» **LIFESPAN**
At least 40 years

» **SIZE**
About 50 ft long

» **WEIGHT**
Up to 40 tons

» **DIET**
Tiny shrimp called amphipods, which live on the sea floor

» **CONSERVATION STATUS**
Least Concern. About 15,000 to 20,000 in the world.

» **LOCATION**
North Pacific Ocean

DID YOU KNOW?

* Instead of a fin on its back, a gray whale has a row of lumps shaped like the knuckles of your hand.

* Many gray whales have long scars and bits of fin missing from attacks by killer whales.

* A swimming gray whale may stop and stick its head up out of the water to look around. This is called "spy-hopping."

* Feeding gray whales are easily spotted from airplanes because they stir up great trails of muddy water.

TOOTHED WHALES

There are at least 76 species of
toothed whales, which includes
dolphins, and most of them are much
smaller than baleen whales. All have
real teeth and only one blowhole.
They have a fatty organ—a "melon"—
in their head that focuses special
click sounds used for echolocation.

& DOLPHINS

SPERM WHALES

family name	number of species
Physeteridae	**1**

Sperm whales have a massive, square-shaped head that is so big it takes up a third of the whole body. All their teeth are in the narrow lower jaw under the head and each tooth slots into a socket in the huge top jaw. Most adult males hunt on their own, but groups of females and young can be seen resting at the surface before diving deep for their food.

Sperm whale

EXAMPLE: SPERM WHALE *(Physeter Macrocephalus)*

DEEP DIVERS

Giant squid are a favorite food of sperm whales, but they have to dive deep to find them. No one knows exactly how deep, but probably down to at least 1-2 miles. Sperm whales can hold their breath for two hours, but 45 minutes is more usual. The triangular-shaped tail "flukes" are lifted high in the air as they dive.

Scar

A CLOSER LOOK

» LIFESPAN
Over 70 years

» SIZE
40 ft (females)
60 ft (males)

» WEIGHT
Up to 57 tons

» DIET
Squid, octopus, deep-sea fish

» CONSERVATION STATUS
Unknown, possibly about 360,000. Vulnerable and protected from commercial hunting.

» LOCATION
Worldwide in all oceans. Only close to land where there are deep underwater canyons

DID YOU KNOW?

★ Sperm whales have the largest brain of any creature that has ever lived on Earth.

★ Female sperm whales live in pods of 15-20 whales. Mothers protect their babies from killer whales by forming a circle with the babies in the middle.

★ Sperm whales have lots of wrinkles and scars on their skin.

★ Pygmy and dwarf sperm whales are related to sperm whales but belong to a different family (*Kogiidae*).

NARWHAL & BELUGA

family name	number of species
Monodontidae	**2**

Narwhal and beluga are two unusual whales that live among the pack ice around the edges of the Arctic Ocean. They have a small, bulging head and a thick body with rolls of fat called blubber to keep them warm in freezing waters. When they surface, white beluga are easy to spot from the air, but speckled gray narwhal and the dark gray calves of both species do not show up so well.

Narwhal

UNICORNS OF THE SEA

Male narwhal have an elegant, twisted tusk on their heads, just like a mythical unicorn. They use this to show off and fight to win the best females.

A recent film taken from a drone has shown that narwhal also use their tusk to hit and stun fish, before sucking them into their mouths.

A CLOSER LOOK

» LIFESPAN
25-50 years

» SIZE
Body 13-16 ft; tusk up to 9 ft

» WEIGHT
Up to 1.5 tons

» DIET
Fish, shrimp, and squid

» CONSERVATION STATUS
Near Threatened. About 50,000 in the world.

» LOCATION
Arctic Ocean, especially Baffin Bay.

DID YOU KNOW?

★ Narwhal only have two teeth. In males, the left one grows through the top lip and becomes the tusk. Sometimes both teeth form tusks, and a few females grow a short tusk.

★ Narwhals live in groups. They are often seen in groups of 2-10, but hundreds have been spotted together before.

★ Unlike most other whales, beluga have flexible lips and can change the expression on their faces. They also make a greater number of different noises than any other whale.

★ Canadian Inuit people rely on narwhal for food, skins, and tusks for carving.

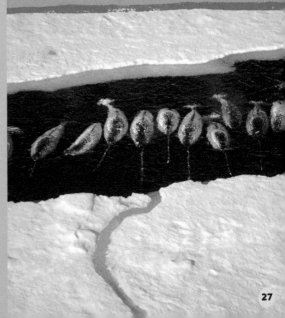

BEAKED WHALES

family name
Ziphiidae

number of species
22

Beaked whales live and hunt in deep water and are not seen very often. They look like oversized dolphins, but only have a small fin on their back, which is near their tail. Most of them have a long beak and a hump—called a melon—on the top of their head. They also have two throat grooves under their head and no notch in their tail fin.

Cuvier's beaked whale

SCARRING

You can tell male from female beaked whales because adult males are covered in long scratches. Males only have one pair of teeth that stick out from the front or sides of their lower jaw—known as a beak—and are used to fight other males. Beaked whales often have lots of circular scars where cookie-cutter sharks have bitten them.

A CLOSER LOOK

» **LIFESPAN**
Unknown but at least 25 years

» **SIZE**
Up to 23 ft

» **WEIGHT**
Up to about 3 tons

» **DIET**
Mostly deep sea squid and some fish

» **CONSERVATION STATUS**
Least Concern. The most common beaked whale.

» **LOCATION**
All oceans in deep water

DID YOU KNOW?

★ One Cuvier's beaked whale tracker recorded a dive of 10,000 feet, which is a record for any mammal. Another stayed underwater for 138 minutes.

★ This whale's mouth curves upward, which makes it look like it is smiling.

★ Scientists know quite a lot about Cuvier's and Blainville's beaked whales, but not much about many others. There are probably new species waiting to be found!

★ Like other beaked whales, barnacles often grow on their sticking-out teeth.

Scarring

OCEAN DOLPHINS

family name	number of species
Delphinidae	**38**

Ocean dolphins spend a lot of time near the surface an
can be spotted from the shore and from ships. These sle
and streamlined animals have a curved fin in the middle
their back and slender, pointed flippers. Most have blac
or gray backs, but some have pretty cream-and-white
patterns on their sides. There are many different specie
so let's look at the three most famous...

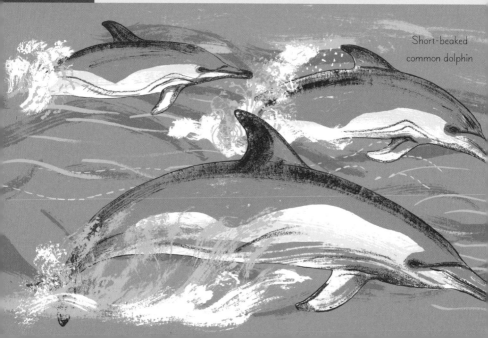

Short-beaked
common dolphin

XAMPLE 1: SHORT-BEAKED COMMON DOLPHIN *(Delphinus delphis)*

ACROBATICS

Ocean dolphins are fast, acrobatic swimmers. They leap in and out of the water as they travel along. This way they can keep going and breathe through their blowhole each time they surface. Sometimes they even ride along the bow waves of ships. They can also jump, somersault, and slap the water with their flippers and tail.

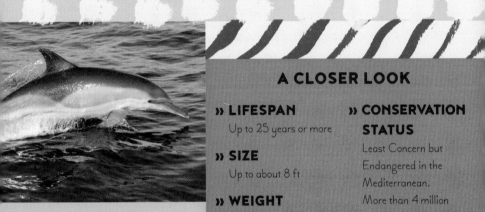

DID YOU KNOW?

★ Most ocean dolphins travel in small groups, but some schools of short-beaked common dolphins have as many as 10,000 individuals.

★ This dolphin is playful and social and will even swim with pilot whales.

★ The smallest ocean dolphin (Heaviside's) is half the size of the common dolphin. The largest species (orca) is four times bigger.

★ The common dolphin is one of the most colorful dolphins. Its panels of yellow and white form an hourglass shape on its side.

A CLOSER LOOK

» LIFESPAN
Up to 25 years or more

» SIZE
Up to about 8 ft

» WEIGHT
Up to 400 lb

» DIET
Shoals of small fish and squid

» CONSERVATION STATUS
Least Concern but Endangered in the Mediterranean. More than 4 million worldwide.

» LOCATION
Atlantic and Pacific Oceans

OCEAN DOLPHINS

EXAMPLE 2: COMMON BOTTLENOSE DOLPHIN *(Tursiops trunca*

The bottlenose dolphin is one of the best known of all dolphins. Wild bottlenose dolphins usually live near the coast, though some travel right out into the middle of the ocean. They are very curious and will often swim over to interact with boats, bathers, and divers. They are large, strong dolphins with a stout beak that is tough enough to ram dangerous predators such as sharks or killer whales.

Common bottlenose dolphin

DOLPHIN TALK

Most dolphins can make sounds and bottlenose dolphins are especially good at this. At the surface, they snort air out through their blowhole and make different whistles, clicks, and chirps by changing the size and shape of the blowhole. The blowhole is kept closed underwater, so then they make noises using special air sacs in their head. Bottlenose dolphins may be able to recognize each other from their calls.

A CLOSER LOOK

» LIFESPAN
Up to 50 years

» SIZE
7-14 ft

» WEIGHT
1,400 lb maximum

» DIET
Many different fish, and some shrimp, crabs, and squid

» CONSERVATION STATUS
Least Concern. Unknown number but at least 600,000 worldwide.

» LOCATION
Atlantic, Pacific, and Indian Oceans mostly near coasts

DID YOU KNOW?

★ Bottlenose dolphins signal to each other by slapping their tail or flippers on the water or on their bodies. This works like us clapping our hands.

★ These dolphins sometimes use long streams of very loud underwater clicks to frighten other dolphins away or to keep their young in order.

★ Some family groups live permanently in one place and can always be found in their chosen bay or estuary.

★ All dolphins swallow their prey whole without chewing it.

OCEAN DOLPHINS

EXAMPLE 3: ORCA OR KILLER WHALE *(Orcinus orca)*

This giant ocean dolphin is often called a killer whale because it can kill and eat almost any other large animal in the sea. Orcas have a mouthful of large, pointed teeth as thick as your thumb and can easily crunch through tough skin. At the surface, orcas cruise slowly along with their huge dorsal fin sticking three or even six feet up into the air. They have a unique black–and–white color pattern.

Killer whale

CLOSE FAMILIES

Most killer whales live in large family groups called pods. The individuals all travel together and help each other when hunting their prey. Pods can be small or have 50 or more members. In some "resident" pods in the North Pacific, calves stay and grow up in the pod after they are born and may never leave. Sometimes several pods travel together as a larger community.

DID YOU KNOW?

* Some scientists now think that there may be several different species of orca. They have slightly different color patterns, and ways of feeding.

* Like some other dolphins, orca calves are a different color than the adults. Their white patches are a rusty orange color until they are a few months old.

* Killer whales are dangerous animals but do not usually attack people unless they are provoked.

* Most dolphins swallow their prey whole, but when orcas attack large mammals like whales, they eat it in bits.

A CLOSER LOOK

» **LIFESPAN**
Males 50-60 years, females up to 90 years

» **SIZE**
Over 30 ft

» **WEIGHT**
Up to about 10 tons

» **DIET**
Marine mammals, fish, sharks, penguins, turtles

» **CONSERVATION STATUS**
Data Deficient; some local populations are Endangered. Unknown but at least 50,000 worldwide.

» **LOCATION**
Worldwide in all oceans

PORPOISES

family name
Phocoenidae

number of species
7

Porpoises are much more difficult to see than dolphins, because they usually swim quietly along in small groups and they rarely leap or splash. They live along coastlines and prefer the calm water in shallow bays and estuaries. Most are quite small, but rather fat because they have lots of blubber to keep them warm. They have a blunt nose instead of a beak and only a small fin on their back.

Harbor porpoise

SPECIAL TEETH

Porpoises have teeth that are especially good at slicing through fish, and they eat at least 20 different sorts. Each tooth is shaped like a miniature spade with the biting end flattened into a wide, sharp blade. They can also crunch into shellfish, but like dolphins, they do not chew their food.

A CLOSER LOOK

» **LIFESPAN**
10-24 years

» **SIZE**
Up to 7 ft

» **WEIGHT**
Up to 160 lb

» **DIET**
Small fish and squid

» **CONSERVATION STATUS**
Least Concern. At least 700,000 worldwide.

» **LOCATION**
North Pacific, North Atlantic, and Arctic

DID YOU KNOW?

★ Harbor porpoises are very shy creatures that are difficult to spot. Scientists have much more to learn about them because they are hard to find and study.

★ Fishing nets are a big threat to harbor porpoises. Their numbers are declining because thousands are caught by mistake every year.

★ They are one of the smallest cetaceans.

★ Harbor porpoises come up every few minutes to breathe. As they do this, they make a funny noise that sounds like a sneeze.

RIVER DOLPHINS

family name
Platanistidae and Iniidae

number of species
3

A muddy river is a very unusual place for a dolphin to live, and only a few species live all the time in this water. River dolphins have a very long snout, tiny eyes, and large flippers shaped like paddles. They swim slowly in the murky water and find their way by using echolocation, just as bats do in the dark. True river dolphins are only found in tropical rivers in South America, India, and Pakistan.

Amazon river dolphin

EXAMPLE: AMAZON RIVER DOLPHIN OR BOTO *(Inia geoffrensis)*

FIRST FLOODING

In the rainy season, the Amazon river floods into the forest that lines its banks. The river dolphins swim in among the tree trunks searching for fish.

They have very bendy necks and flexible bodies so they can twist between submerged branches. Ocean dolphins have stiff necks and would not be able to do this.

DID YOU KNOW?

★ The Amazon river dolphin is also called the pink dolphin because it has large areas of skin with no gray pigment. Those living in sunny stretches of river seem to have more pigment.

★ The Tucuxi is a small ocean dolphin that also lives in the Amazon river, but it does not move into the surrounding forest when it floods.

★ The Baiji was a true river dolphin that lived in the Yangtze river in China. Now scientists think that it is extinct.

★ Some ocean dolphins, such as the Irrawaddy dolphin, occasionally swim up rivers.

A CLOSER LOOK

» **LIFESPAN**
Unknown

» **SIZE**
Up to 9 ft

» **WEIGHT**
Up to 450 lb

» **DIET**
Around 40 sorts of fish including piranha and crustaceans

» **CONSERVATION STATUS**
Data Deficient; many threats. Unknown number, possibly 15,000.

» **LOCATION**
Amazon and Orinoco Rivers, South America

DUGONGS

&

MANATEES

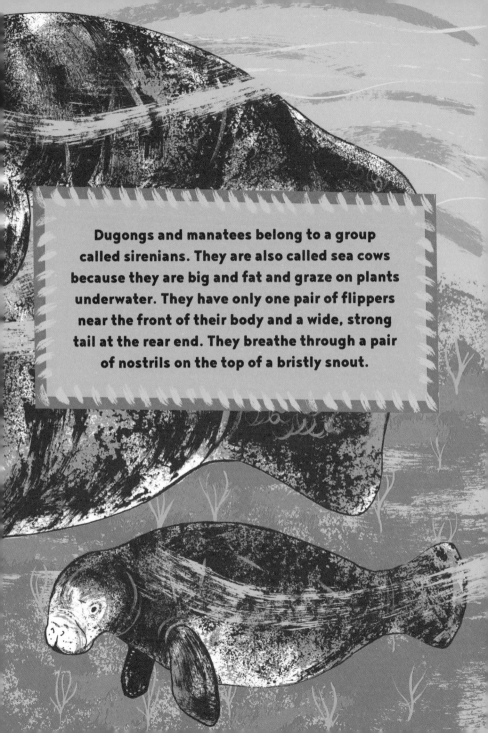

Dugongs and manatees belong to a group called sirenians. They are also called sea cows because they are big and fat and graze on plants underwater. They have only one pair of flippers near the front of their body and a wide, strong tail at the rear end. They breathe through a pair of nostrils on the top of a bristly snout.

DUGONGS

family name	number of species
Dugongidae	**1**

Dugongs look like fat dolphins, but have a big, drooping snout with a whiskery mouth and thick lips. They swim with their tail but use their large flippers to pull themselves along the seabed while they graze. They live along the coasts of about 40 different countries, but nowadays the best places to see dugongs are in the clear waters around northern Australia.

Dugong

EXAMPLE: DUGONG *(Dugong dugon)*

GRAZING

Dugongs spend most of the day munching on seagrass, just like cows grazing in a meadow on land. They can eat as much as 100 pounds of seagrass a day. Every few minutes, dugongs have to stop eating and come to the surface to breathe. Their nostrils are on the top of the snout so they can take a breath without lifting their head out of the water.

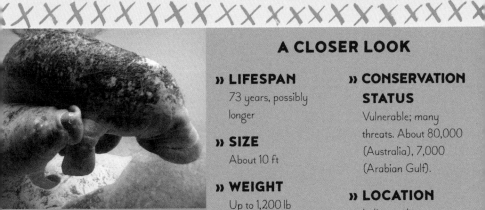

A CLOSER LOOK

» **LIFESPAN**
73 years, possibly longer

» **SIZE**
About 10 ft

» **WEIGHT**
Up to 1,200 lb

» **DIET**
Seagrass

» **CONSERVATION STATUS**
Vulnerable; many threats. About 80,000 (Australia), 7,000 (Arabian Gulf).

» **LOCATION**
Indian and western Pacific Oceans (Indo-Pacific)

DID YOU KNOW?

* Like manatees, dugongs close their nostrils underwater. They can hold their breath for 10 minutes.

* Juvenile golden trevally fish follow dugongs and snap up small creatures disturbed from the mud.

* Dugongs are related to elephants and have small tusks that stick out of their mouths.

* Seagrass beds grow in shallow water and are easily damaged by boat anchors, pollution and storms. Without them, dugongs and many other animals can't survive.

MANATEES

family name	number of species
Trichechidae	**3**

Manatees have big, fat bodies with wrinkled rough skin like an elephant or a hippo. They are similar in shape to dugongs but have a flat, round tail. They live a lazy life swimming slowly along coasts and in rivers in the warm tropics and spend half their time asleep, while they digest their huge meals of waterplants. They have a very long gut—up to 130 feet—to help with this.

American (West Indian)
manatee

EXAMPLE: AMERICAN MANATEE *(Trichechus manatus)*

WARMING UP

American manatees in Florida have learned that the water released from power stations warms up nearby rivers in winter. So when it gets cold, many of them crowd near the outfalls and into warm freshwater springs. Others still swim many hundreds of miles south to spend the winter, returning in spring.

A CLOSER LOOK

» **LIFESPAN**
60–70 years

» **SIZE**
Up to 13 ft

» **WEIGHT**
Up to 3,500 lb

» **DIET**
Underwater plants including water hyacinths and seagrass

» **CONSERVATION STATUS**
Vulnerable; about 4,000. Numbers are going down.

» **LOCATION**
Coasts, rivers, and estuaries from Florida to central Brazil

DID YOU KNOW?

★ Manatees have less than ten large teeth near the back of their jaws, and as these wear out, they are pushed out by new ones growing behind. They get through about 80 teeth in their lifetime.

★ Like other sea cows, American manatees have only one baby at a time and feed it for about two years.

★ Manatees usually have many scars and cuts and American manatees in Florida are often seriously hurt by passing speedboats.

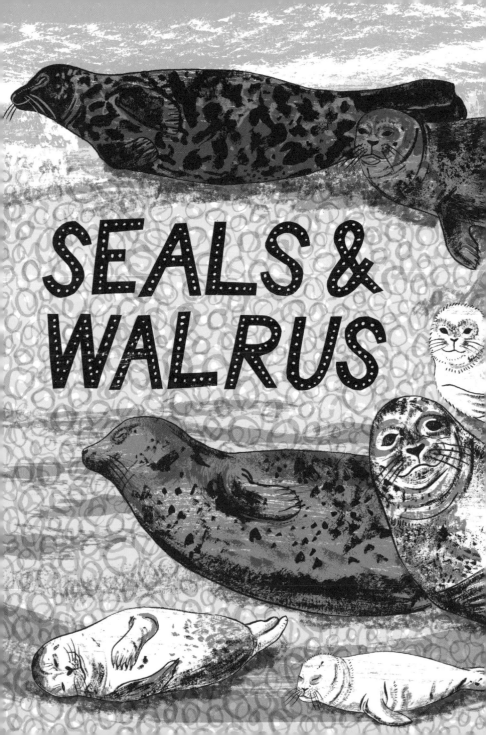

SEALS &
WALRUS

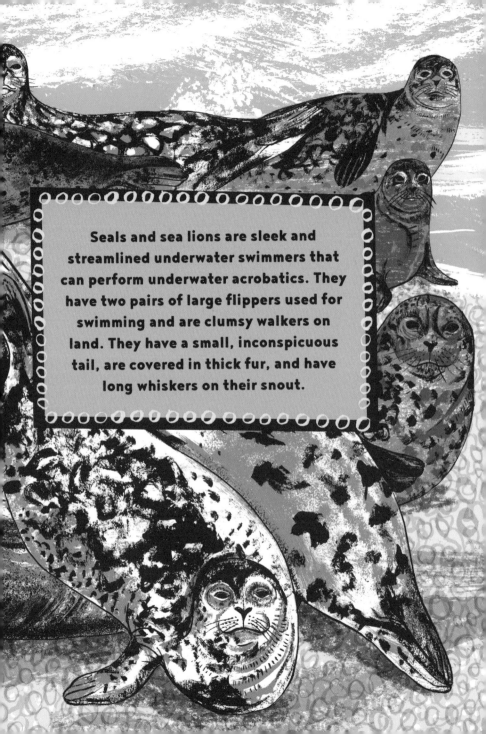

Seals and sea lions are sleek and streamlined underwater swimmers that can perform underwater acrobatics. They have two pairs of large flippers used for swimming and are clumsy walkers on land. They have a small, inconspicuous tail, are covered in thick fur, and have long whiskers on their snout.

EARED SEALS

family name	number of species
Otariidae	**15**

Sea lions and fur seals are called eared seals because they have a little ear flap next to the opening of each ear. They are easy to see on land because they like to live in large groups and there are always some propped up on their front flippers looking around. They can walk and even run on land because, unlike earless seals, they can turn their rear flippers to face forward.

California sea lion

INTELLIGENCE

When they are not hunting for fish, California sea lions love to play and will swim, twist, and chase each other underwater and make acrobatic leaps above the surface. This ability helps them to escape predators such as orcas. They are very intelligent and are often trained to perform acrobatic tricks in captivity.

A CLOSER LOOK

» **LIFESPAN**
Unknown but at least 25 years

» **SIZE**
8 ft

» **WEIGHT**
Up to 860 lb

» **DIET**
Many different fish

» **CONSERVATION STATUS**
Least Concern; population increasing.

» **LOCATION**
Eastern North Pacific from Mexico to the Gulf of Alaska

DID YOU KNOW?

★ Adult males of most species have a mane of fur around their head, but the California sea lion does not.

★ Seals make lots of noises, and male California sea lions bark repeatedly—a lot like a dog does.

★ Like other seals, huge numbers of this sea lion gather together in "rookeries" to breed on special beaches.

★ Sea lions can sleep in the water, with only half their brain asleep. They float with a front and rear flipper held up in the air. Fur seals touch these together.

TRUE SEALS

family name	number of species
Phocidae	**18**

While they are expert swimmers, true seals are very ungainly on land. In the water, they sweep their powerful hind flippers from side to side just as a fish does with its tail. On land these flippers trail behind them and they drag themselves forward using their front flippers. True seals have excellent hearing even though they are sometimes called earless seals. Their ears are almost invisible with just a tiny entrance hole behind each eye.

Harbor seal

SWIMMING

Baby harbor seals can swim almost right away after they are born. They shed their white baby fur while they are inside their mother, and their new fur is pale gray and waterproof. They need to swim quickly because they are often born on sand banks where the tide comes back in soon after they are born.

A CLOSER LOOK

» **LIFESPAN**
25 years (males)
35 years (females)

» **SIZE**
Up to 6 ft

» **WEIGHT**
Up to 330 lb

» **DIET**
Fish, squid, octopus, crabs, and other crustaceans

» **CONSERVATION STATUS**
Least Concern. About 500,000 worldwide.

» **LOCATION**
Near coasts in N. Atlantic, North Pacific, and Arctic

DID YOU KNOW?

★ Some harbor seals in San Francisco Bay have red fur. Iron stirred up from the seabed colors their fur so they look rusty.

★ Harbor seals often swim up rivers.

★ Harbor seals can stay underwater for up to 30 minutes, but an average dive is around three minutes

★ True seals produce milk that is 40-60% fat so the young grow very quickly. harbor seal milk is about 50% fat.

WALRUS

family name
Odobenidae

Walrus are nearly the biggest and certainly the fattest seal. They have a huge, blubbery body with thick folds of skin but hardly any fur. Most of the time, they lie around on sea ice or on remote seashores, packed close together in untidy heaps. Their two curved tusks are extra-long canine teeth that keep on growing all their life. These can be three feet long in adult males!

Walrus

USING TUSKS

Walruses use their long tusks to pull themselves up onto slippery sea ice after a dive. When a walrus is feeding, it uses fleshy mouth pads with a mustache of stiff bristles to find and dig out buried food, which it uncovers with squirts of water. Males use their extra-long tusks to fight each other for females.

Tusks

A CLOSER LOOK

» LIFESPAN
About 40 years

» SIZE
Up to 11.5 ft

» WEIGHT
Up to 3,500 lb

» DIET
Clams, worms, crabs, and many other invertebrates

» CONSERVATION STATUS
Vulnerable. About 225,000 worldwide.

» LOCATION
Arctic Ocean and subarctic

DID YOU KNOW?

★ A walrus can save heat by slowing down the flow of blood to its skin when it dives into cold water.

★ Back on land, the walrus changes from a pale gray color to pinkish brown as the warm blood returns.

★ Walruses can float and sleep with their heads above water by filling two pouches in their throat with air.

★ Climate change is melting the sea ice where walruses rest. This is the main threat to their survival.

OTTERS

Most otters live in freshwater rivers; only the sea otter and the marine otter get all their food from the sea. All otters belong to one family, which also includes many land mammals such as skunks and badgers. They have four feet with strong claws and can run on land. A long tail helps them swim, and thick fur keeps them warm.

SEA AND MARINE OTTERS

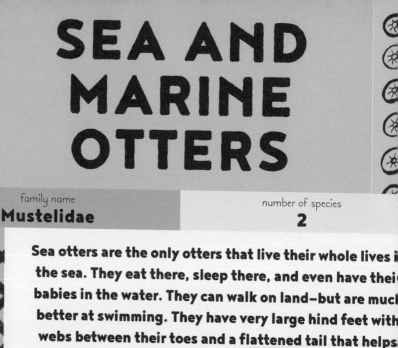

family name	number of species
Mustelidae	**2**

Sea otters are the only otters that live their whole lives in the sea. They eat there, sleep there, and even have their babies in the water. They can walk on land—but are much better at swimming. They have very large hind feet with webs between their toes and a flattened tail that helps them to swim. River otters sometimes visit the sea to hunt for fish, but marine otters always hunt in the sea.

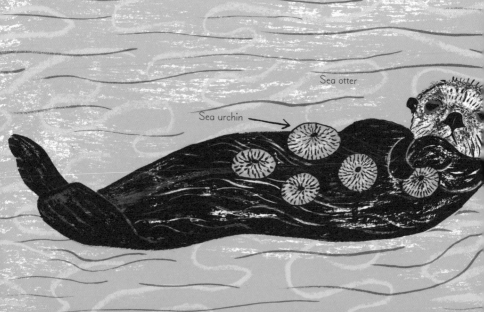

Sea otter

Sea urchin

EXAMPLE: SEA OTTER *(Enhydra lutris)*

FEEDING

A hungry sea otter dives down to search for mollusks and crabs and uses its long whiskers and nose to find them. Sea otters have tough pads on their front paws and can even pick up prickly sea urchins. If the food is too tough to crush with its sharp teeth, it balances a rock on its tummy and smashes its prey onto it.

A CLOSER LOOK

» **LIFESPAN**
Probably 15-20 years

» **SIZE**
Up to 5 ft

» **WEIGHT**
Up to 100 lb

» **DIET**
Invertebrates such as clams, abalones, crabs, and urchins

» **CONSERVATION STATUS**
Endangered and declining. About 126,000.

» **LOCATION**
Pacific coasts of North America, Aleutian Islands (Alaska), and Kamchatka (Russia)

DID YOU KNOW?

★ Sea otters have much thicker fur than other otters. Each square centimeter of skin has around 150,000 hairs.

★ They can carry rocks and food in loose folds of skin under their armpits.

★ While a mother hunts for food, she may leave her baby wrapped in floating kelp (seaweed) held up by air sacs in the plant.

★ Sea otters spend a lot of time swimming slowly on their backs. They turn over if they want to swim faster.

BEARS

There are eight species of bears in one family, *Ursidae.* They all live on land except for the polar bear. Land bears will eat almost anything, but polar bears get almost all their food by hunting for seals and other marine animals in the sea and from sea ice.

POLAR BEAR

family name	number of marine species
Ursidae	**1**

Although Arctic winters are bitterly cold, this is the best time of year for polar bears, because they live most of their life out on the ice covering the Arctic Ocean. They have two layers of thick fur to keep them warm and only small ears and a short tail, which saves heat loss. Huge front paws with webs between the toes help them to swim and to walk on thin ice.

Polar bear

HUNTING ON ICE

Polar bears do almost all their hunting from the Arctic ice. They walk, swim, and scramble for miles sniffing out and stalking seals. Some wait for hours by holes where seals come up to breathe, then pounce, and pull the seal onto the ice to eat it. Climate change is making it harder for them to hunt because in summer the ice now retreats farther and faster offshore.

A CLOSER LOOK

» LIFESPAN
15-18 years, sometimes 30 years

» SIZE
Up to 8 ft (males)
6.5 ft (females)

» WEIGHT
Up to 1,700 lb (males),
700 lb (females)

» DIET
Ringed Seals; other seals, Beluga, Narwhal

» CONSERVATION STATUS
Vulnerable; about 26,000.

» LOCATION
Around the coastline and islands of the Arctic

DID YOU KNOW?

★ Baby polar bears weigh only 1 pound when they are born in winter in snow dens. When mother and cubs emerge in spring, they weigh about 20 pounds.

★ Polar bears have been tracked swimming 100 miles and one was spotted 200 miles from land.

★ They can run at 25 miles per hour and have small bumps on their foot pads help them grip the ice.

★ The skin under a polar bear's white fur is actually black.

★ Polar bears can smell a seal hidden 3 feet below the snow.

Foot pads

INDEX

Photographic acknowledgments: p.17 (top) Blue whale blowing at the surface © Alamy Stock Photo; p.17 (bottom) Blue whale © Alamy Stock Photo; p.19 (bottom) Humpback whale bubble net feeding © Alamy Stock Photo; p.25 Sperm whale © Alamy Stock Photo; p.27 Narwhal pod in pack © Alamy Stock Photo; p.27 Narwhals showing tusks above water © Alamy Stock Photo; p.29 (top) Cuvier's beaked whale © Alamy Stock Photo; p.29 (bottom) Cuvier's beaked whale breaching © Alamy Stock Photo; p.37 (top) Harbor porpose © Alamy Stock Photo; All other photographs © Shutterstock.

Brimming with creative inspiration, how-to projects, and useful information to enrich your everyday life, Quarto Knows is a favorite destination for those pursuing their interests and passions. Visit our site and dig deeper with our books into your area of interest: Quarto Creates, Quarto Cooks, Quarto Homes, Quarto Lives, Quarto Drives, Quarto Explores, Quarto Gifts, or Quarto Kids.

Pocket Guide to Whales, Dolphins, and Other Marine Mammals © 2018 Quarto Publishing plc. Text by Frances Dipper. Illustrations © 2018 Alice Pattullo.

First Published in 2018 by Lincoln Children's Books, an imprint of The Quarto Group. 400 First Avenue North, Suite 400, Minneapolis, MN 55401, USA. T (612) 344-8100 F (612) 344-8692 **www.QuartoKnows.com**

The right of Alice Pattullo to be identified as the illustrator and Frances Dipper to be identified as the author of this work has been asserted by them in accordance with the Copyright, Designs and Patents Act, 1988 (United Kingdom).

Published in association with the Natural History Museum, London.

ISBN 978-1-78603-109-9

Illustrated with brush and Indian ink, collaged hand-painted patterns, and digital composition. Set in Pistacho Soft, Noyh A Bistro, and hand-lettered text

Published by Rachel Williams and Jenny Broom
Designed by Nicola Price
Edited by Katy Flint
Production by Jenny Cundill

Manufactured in Dongguan, China in TL052018

9 8 7 6 5 4 3 2 1

FSC
www.fsc.org

MIX
Paper from responsible sources
FSC® C104723